THE IRRELEVANT SONG

by Brian Patten

LITTLE JOHNNY'S CONFESSION
NOTES TO THE HURRYING MAN
THE ELEPHANT AND THE FLOWER

THE IRRELEVANT SONG

by Brian Patten

London
George Allen and Unwin Ltd
Ruskin House Museum Street

First published in 1971

© Brian Patten 1971

ISBN 0 04 821027 7 Cased
        0 04 821028 5 Paper

Some of these poems have previously appeared in
small press magazines and in limited editions by
Turret Books, and The Sceptre Press. A longer
version of 'The Albatross Ramble', intended more for
the voice than the page, was published in *The
London Magazine*, and a different version of the
poem, 'The Irrelevant Song' was first published in
The Poetry Review. Acknowledgements and thanks
are due to the Arts Council of Great Britain and to
others who took an interest in these poems.

Printed in Great Britain
in 9 point Univers type leaded
by Unwin Brothers Limited, Woking and London.

For Mary

CONTENTS

I

THE IRRELEVANT SONG

'Already in the wood the light grass has darkened.
Like a necklace of deaths the flowers hug the ground;
Their scents, once magically known,
Seem now irretrievable.'

THE IRRELEVANT SONG

William wrote love songs . . .
In cafés, in ballrooms,
On seaside proms before the people had risen.
He translated all that the birds said.
He made his home in often forests;
With a twig and ink from mushrooms
He would write on leaves,
On bark cut from tree-trunks.
He was your love, was mine;
Was her lover, and his lover;
The total lover was William.
His songs, lyrical and splendid, became rivers.

Yet however early he had risen
The spaces beside him
Would be left vacant.
No shy ladies hurried down his morning pathway.
No small winter heel-prints dug into the soft ice.

Still inside him most mornings frosty light gathered,
His loss grew branches,
Across his tongue
The world's tastes skated.

William, lost in downpours,
Dreamt in forests:
Of simple
Scented
Singing
And repetitive bodies.
They pushed through the bushes to where he sat.
Hunched in the damp tree-roots,
Loose memory swilled about him.

William dreamt of bodies.
Mostly of long bodies.
The spines fur covered.
The skin by touch tightened.
Swan-like, lazy.

He wrote often of small breasted ladies met in village stations,
Of their healthy red noses,
Their legs in cord trousers.

He wrote of things that brought tears to the eyes of sparrows.
Even the crows built their nests low down
That they might listen.
Puffins worked their way inland through obscure rivers.
The sea had told them of William.
They listened from the damp bushes.
He wrote many love songs . . .
On trains going nowhere,
On the flyleafs of bibles.

In his garden he grew flowers that smelt of warm bodies.
He mated bushes,
Bred a rose the colour of
The only drawers he remembered.
In the animal and bird world he became famous.
Whales deep in oceans held literary conversations.
William, they said, was the great Human Lover.
O true mammal,
King of the Cloudy Kingdom,
O Poet Of The Multitude Beyond The Hill That Never Listens.

He wears a lion's mane in bed.
Wakes in golden fur.

William worked hard against his senses closing.
The belief that his touch was everlasting,
That cheeks, cool and loaded with scent, silence and days glowing
Would always stay turned towards him
Had not left him.
In such belief his light was founded.

Idiotic William
Passed 'teens
Passed twenties
Pruned his heart.

And so a story changes . . .

One morning he was visited by the Daughter of Sorrow.
Her name was Sympathy Unbuttoned.
Her eyes were green as meadows.
Small spiders nested in her curls.
Her breasts were non-existent.

They wandered together
Daily,
Weekly,
Wandered in woodland making new pathways.

Where the trees thinned out,
Where the deep rivers shallowed,
They found estuaries,
Mudflats,
Herring-gulls,
The awkward sandpipers,
The small boats stranded in which
None drowned ever.

Thin William spoke his verses;
His lady listened.
Breathless and breastless
She listened in wonder.

When in winter his tongue was frozen
And on his cheeks
Rain also had frozen
She watched his village girls,
His proms,
His ballroom and cafés
Pass in icy procession from eyelid to cheek-bone.

For her he tried to protect the rivers.
They went underground.
Lost in bramble and cool stone darkness
They escaped him.

He asked the birds for more song,
More variety.
More! More!
Their throats dried up.
Now all day they sleep in their branches.

Why are the fields barren?
For her William has gathered in the flowers,
Frightened elst the evening freezes them.

The cottage is in darkness.
He has closed the shutters else
Hailstones smash the windows.

His lady is pleased.

Good morning Sympathy,
Besides William's dream-land
What other countries have you invaded?
Crouching in fields where late couples are lying,
A pale stork moving in shadows.
On your way into light did you notice
The blackbirds frozen in their nests,
The girls waking in early rooms,
Possessed by dreams that would not suit you?

Didn't the larks warn you
That nothing is for ever?
That in the stoat's den the rabbit leaves no message?
Didn't the tree's branches warn you
Blown leaves don't mind parting?
The sad endings you pursue
Are but things completed.

14

The yawning hares in a landscape of heather
Do not wonder if they will outlive one another
Nor why the scented winds
Splash down among them.

William wrote long songs . . .
But the birds in the woodland,
The whales in the oceans,
The puffins and sparrows
And awkward sandpipers
Lost faith.

His first songs,
The loneliest,
The loveliest,
Fled into an irretrievable country.
The city hardly found him.
Nature soon forgot him.

In the Daughter of Sadness,
Breastless in forests,
All his songs had gathered.
In so single a lady
No great dream could be founded;
Among the curls and the spiders
His eyes had rested.

The songs grew dreamless,
The pathways clotted,
A memory of light leapt about in the forests,
And the Daughter of Sadness
Just ironed out his shadows
For William to wear
On his way through the seasons.

And so with this a story's ended:
William woke,
He rose from out a lovesick shadow.

When field, lake, river, mist and valley
Closed down its wonder,
In a peculiar season
Caught between dyings,
William disowned her.
From his sight then
The blurred lights drifted.

Rain drowned the valleys;
In a catacomb of soaking grass
Grounded birds were crying.
His dark was internal but soon
It stepped outwards.
Into his songs there leaked
More awkward celebrations;
Messages sent via lark and rose
Relinquished any meaning.
What was left was yet to be encountered.

William wrote love songs,
Where the thin grasses had perished,
Where the night hugged its own shapes
And love hugged its habits.

II

WILLIAM'S SONGS

'Because joy and sorrow must finally unite
And the small heart beat of sparrow
Be heard above jet-roar
I will sing,
Not of tomorrow's impossible paradise
But of what now radiates.'

AT FOUR O'CLOCK IN THE MORNING

As all is temporary and is changeable,
So in this bed my love you lie,
Temporary beyond imaginings;
Trusting and certain, in present time you rest,
A world completed.

Yet already are the windows freaked with dawn;
Shrill song reminds
Each of a separate knowledge;
Shrill light might make of love
A weight both false and monstrous.

So hush; enough words are used:
We know how blunt can grow such phrases as
Only children use without
Awareness of their human weight.

There is no need to impose upon feelings
Yesterday's echo.
I love you true enough;
Beyond this, nothing is now expected.

These songs were begun one winter
When on a window thick with frost
Her finger drew
A map of all possible directions,
When her body was one possibility among
Arbitrary encounters
And loneliness sufficient to warrant
A meeting of opposites.

How easily forgotten then
What was first felt—
An anchor lifted from the blood,
Sensations intense as any lunatic's,
Ruined by unaccustomary events,
Let drop because of weariness.

EARLY IN THE EVENING

I met her early in the evening
The cars were going home
I was twenty-four and dreaming
My head was full of shadows her brightness cancelled
Beneath her dress her breasts were pushing
It was early in the evening
Spring was only a few streets away
In the closed parks the leaves were trying
The pubs had nothing to give us
Early in the evening
When the street railings were burning
There was nothing much to do but to be together

She drifted into sleep early in the evening
Her head was on the pillow
The sun that fell about her
Drifted in the window
Early in the evening
Some birds still sang on rooftops
Their hearts could have fitted into egg-cups
It was early in the evening
The sky was going purple
Her dress lay on a chair by the window
Early in the evening she had shook it from her
She was awake and was dreaming
Her head was free of shadows
Her belly was glowing
I had never imagined a body so loving
I had never imagined a body so golden
Early in the evening we had amazed one another
While the offices were closing
And couples grabbed at telephones
And all the lines were reaching
Early into evening
There was nothing much to do then
And nothing better either

SOMEONE COMING BACK

Now that the summer has emptied
and laughter's warned against possessions,
and the swans have drifted from the rivers,
like one come back from a long journey
no longer certain of his country
or of its tangled past and sorrows,
I am wanting to return to you.

When love-affairs can no longer be distinguished from song
and the warm petals drop without regret,
and our pasts are hung in a dream of ruins,
I am wanting to come near to you.

From now the lark's song has grown visible
and all that was dark is ever possible
and the morning grabs me by the heart and screams,
'O taste me! Taste me please!'

And so I taste. And the tongue is nude,
the eyes awake; the clear blood hums
a tune to which the world might dance;
and love which often lived in vaguer forms
bubbles up through sorrow and laughing, screams:
'O taste me! Taste me please!

BECAUSE THERE WERE NO REVELATIONS AT HAND

Because there were no revelations at hand
And the day being dark
The numerous prophets were elsewhere abiding their time,
I went down to some pool's edge
Where various streams were mixing
And met there a bird with a mouthful of songs.

It fed them to a fish the pool contained;
To the grass also, and then to the trees
It fed its songs.

I wanted to go back and tell them all
Of what had been found.
But the day was dark,
And because no revelations were supposed to be at hand
I stayed there alone.

And standing on the luminous grass
Though there was no prayer in my brain
I spoke with the fish then and found
The lack of anything revealed to be
A revelation of a kind.

THROUGH ALL YOUR ABSTRACT REASONING

Coming back one evening through deserted fields
when the birds, drowsy with sleep,
have all but forgotten you,
you stop, and for one moment jerk alive.

Something has passed through you
that alters and enlightens: O
realization of what has gone and was real;
a bleak and uncoded message whispers
down all the nerves:

'You cared for her! For love you cared I'

Something has passed a finger through
all your abstract reasoning.
From love you sheltered outside of Love but still
the human bit leaked in,
stunned and off-balanced you.

Unprepared, struck so suddenly by another's identity
how can you hold on to any revelation?
You have moved too carefully through your life!
— always the light within you hooded by
your own protecting fingers.

WHEN YOU WAKE TOMORROW

I will give you a poem when you wake tomorrow.
It will be a peaceful poem.
It won't make you sad.
It won't make you miserable.
It will simply be a poem to give you
when you wake tomorrow.

You will find it under your pillow.
When you open the cupboard it will be there.
You will blink in astonishment,
shout out, 'How it trembles!
Its nakedness is startling! How fresh it tastes!'

We will have it for breakfast;
on a table lit by loving,
at a place reserved for wonder.
We will give the world a kissing open
when we wake tomorrow.

We will offer it to the sad landlord out on the balcony.
To the dreamers at the window.
To the hand waving for no particular reason
we will offer it.
An amazing and most remarkable thing,
we will offer it to the whole human race
which walks in us
when we awake tomorrow.

PROBABLY IT IS TOO EARLY IN THE MORNING

Probably it is too early in the morning;
probably you have not yet risen
and the curtains float
like sails against the window.
But whatever, whatever the time, the place, the season,
here I am again at your door,
bringing a bunch of reasons why I should enter.

Probably it is too early inside you yet
for you to gather together what you are and speak;
but whatever, whatever the time, the place, the season,
it is certainly good to have come this far,
to know what I am and not mistrust.

The earth has many hands and doors upon
which these hands are knocking.
There are chairs for some on which to sit
more patient than the rest,
and here I am again, and again am knocking,
holding a fist of primonia,
dressed to kill,
clean dustless and idiotic.
I might be thought mad, insane or stupid;
my belief in you might be totally unfounded;
it might be called utterly romantic,
but what the hell?
Here I am again, and again am knocking.
But probably it is too early;
probably I'm too eager to come rushing towards you,
impatient to share what glows
while there is still
what glows around me.

I bang on the door of the world.
You are asleep behind it.
I bang on the door of the world
as on my own heart a world's been hammering.

THE MORNING'S GOT A SLEEPY HEAD

The morning's got a sleepy head;
it brings parcels of mist, dreams freshly woven,
bright mad gifts it's left on their pillows.

They move together, slower even
than the sun that's above the wood rising.
Learning not to hurry or by-pass
the smallest of sensations,
they go to where lust and tenderness are words,
and words are meaningless.

They've reason for wanting to follow
each other out across the morning,
out to where the hazel opens
and the grass is softest flame.

Forever is one light behind them
that filled a summer,
spilt over into autumn with aches that dropped
when each had lost
the need to care quite hard enough.

Things go too quickly or else they dullen;
quick as the autumn marigold
skates the borders of whitening grass,
things go and nothing seems replaced.
The gap one makes in leaving is not filled.

The morning's got a sleepy head; it brings
parcels of mist, dreams freshly woven,
bright mad tears it's left on their pillows.

SEASON BLOWN

And as to its whereabouts, who knows?
The first love's well vanished,
or sunk at least beneath
an ocean I made, made out

the clouds I became when
all round me bruised itself.

It's not like it where in
the same world's I inherit,
just hidden for the time;
no, it seems well vanished

though traces of what
it wore round itself
are seen at times: tatters
caught on nails, season blown.

HESITANT

He sees beyond her face another face.
It is the one he wants.
He stares at it in amazement;
There is nothing anywhere quite like it.
There is nothing else that's wanted.

She sees beyond his face another face.
It stares at her in amazement.
She stares back, equally amazed.
Just why, she can't quite answer.
She simply wants it.

These faces have been waiting now
A long time to be introduced.
If only the faces in front
Would do something about it.

HER SONG

For no other reason than I love him wholly
I am here; for this one night at least
The world has shrunk to a boyish breast
On which my head, brilliant and exhausted, rests,
And can know of nothing more complete.

Let the dawn assemble all its guilts, its worries
And small doubts that, but for love, would infect
This perfect heart.
I am as far beyond them as the sun.
I am as far beyond them as is possible.

THE OUTGOING SONG

On the warm grass enclosed now
by dull light and silence
your thoughts have fallen. Only

one bird that will insist on jabbering
breaks what calm
has come over you.

All worries, pains, all things that
you owned and were broken by
are reduced to this impassiveness.

For long now no one has brought
giant sorrows; small worries vanish,
spill out from you.

How quiet it is possible to grow!
Then why this want, this reaching out;
why the regrets then? The outgoing song?

WINTER SONG

Coming towards me with no special reason in mind
and your grin big with happiness
that falls, puzzling my plans . . .

The small things that have gathered round me
move now at your
foot's sound on the pathway.

Have I gone crazy then, moving likewise?
What did we ever own that hadn't
the quality of seasons,
their numerous dyings?

With no special reason in mind,
your life full with loving,
your tongue and mouth whispering
across nude snowfalls.

IF WORDS WERE MORE HER MEDIUM
THAN TOUCH

She might have said, if words
Were more her medium than touch:
'Near you is one
Frighteningly real who cannot plan;
Whose heart's a cat from which
Your habits dart like birds;
Who had no weight until you gave
False lust and words like "lost"
A chance to twist
My body into complicated shapes.'

& HEART IS DAFT

Without understanding any pain but that
which inside her anyway is made,
this creature singled out creates
havoc with intelligence. & heart is daft,
is some crazy bird let loose and blind
that slaps against the night and has
never anywhere to go. And when a tongue's
about to speak some nonsense like
'Love is weak, or blind, or both', then comes
this crazy bird, pecks at it like a worm.

32

PARK NOTE

Disgusted by the weight of his own sorrow
I saw one evening
a stranger open wide his coat
and taking out from under it his heart
throw the thing away.

Away over the railings, out across the parks,
across the lakes and the grasses,
as if after much confusion
he had decided not to care but

to move on lightly, carelessly,
amazed and with a grin upon his face
that seemed to say, 'Absurd
how easy that was done.'

I CAUGHT A TRAIN THAT PASSED THE TOWN WHERE YOU LIVED

I caught a train that passed the town where you lived.
On the journey I thought of you.
One evening when the park was soaking
You hid beneath trees, and all round you dimmed itself
as if the earth were lit by gaslight.
We had faith that love would last forever.

I caught a train that passed the town where you lived.

ANGEL WINGS

In the morning I opened the cupboard
and found inside it a pair of wings,
a pair of angel's wings.
I was not naïve enough to believe them real.
I wondered who had left them there.

I took them out the cupboard,
brought them over to the light by the window
and examined them.
You sat in the bed in the light by the window grinning.

'They are mine', you said;
You said that when we met
you'd left them there.

I thought you were crazy.
Your joke embarrassed me.
Nowdays even the mention of the word angel
embarrasses me.

I looked to see how you'd stuck them together.
Looking for glue, I plucked out the feathers.
One by one I plucked them till the bed was littered.

'They are real,' you insisted,
no longer smiling.

And on the pillow your face grew paler.
Your hands reached to stop me but
for some time now I have been embarrassed by the word angel.
For some time now in polite or conservative company
I have checked myself from believing
anything so untouched and yet so touchable
had a chance of existing.

I plucked then
till your face grew even paler;
intent on proving them false
I plucked
and your body grew thinner.
I plucked till you all but vanished.

Soon beside me in the light,
beside the bed in which you were lying
was a mass of torn feathers;
glueless, unstitched, brilliant,
reminiscent of some vague disaster.

In the evening I go out alone now.
You say you can no longer join me.
You say
without wings it is not possible.
You say
ignorance has ruined us,
disbelief has slaughtered.

You stay at home
listening on the radio
to sad and peculiar music,
who fed on belief,
who fed on the light I'd stolen.

Next morning when I opened the cupboard
out stepped a creature,
blank, dull, and too briefly sensual
it brushed out the feathers gloating.

IS THE INNOCENCE OF ANY FLESH SLEEPING

Sleeping beside you I dreamt
I woke beside you;
waking beside you
I thought I was dreaming.

Have you ever slept beside an ocean?
Well yes,
it is like this.

The whole motion of landscapes, of oceans
is within her.
She is
the innocence of any flesh sleeping,
so vulnerable
no protection is needed.

In such times
the heart opens,
contains all there is,
there being no more than her.

In what country she is
I cannot tell.
But knowing —
because there is love
and it blots out all demons —
she is safe,
I can turn,
sleep well beside her.

Waking beside her I am dreaming.
Dreaming of such wakings
I am to all love's senses woken.

IN SOMEPLACE FURTHER ON

In someplace further on you seek
A sympathy that will ignite
A rose with its dying.
A dreamer by whose dreams
Love is made cankerous,
You do not accept easily
Its comings and goings.

As in all things one nature dictates
What energy is needed
To thrive, even among starlight,
So in you more intricate seasons
Plow at the blood.

Some knowledge you tried so hard
Through pain to find
One night while you slept,
Undetected, entered.

Becalmed spider, caught up within your own kill
You do not notice how the web
By a bird is shaken.

THE HEROINE BITCHES

I play my instrument, now like a lark,
perhaps like a nightingale, now perhaps
like the laughter of some girl
ready for anything.

I play, not so much to astonish, but to play.
Then what trickery is it,
what act of absurd fate
that the hero has chosen this moment to arrive?

He will try to overshadow me,
with his love-myth that blossoms on the hearts
of couples too dreamy to notice;
he will attempt to undermine me.

Surely outside the courts, surely in the streets among
the fair-grounds and markets,
among the drunken troubadours and sailors,
I would outshine him?

Heroes would look foolish there.
They belong adrift on oceans
where no one can contradict them and monsters
need not always happen.

What absurdity then that he comes
when I have least need of him?
With my playing I have caught the attention of
the whole crowd
and among them
several I've wanted.

THE TRANSFORMATION

You are no longer afraid.
You watch, still half asleep,
How dawn ignites a room;
His rough head and body curled
In awkward fashion can but please.

His face is puffed with sleep;
His body distant from your own
Has by the dawn been changed,
And what little care you had at first
Within one night has grown.

You smile at how those things that troubled you
Were quick to leave,
At how in their place has come a peace,
A rest once beyond imagining.

Your bodies linked, you hardly dare to move;
A new thought has now obsessed your brain:
'Come the light,
He might again have changed.'
And what you feel
You are quick to name,
And what you feel
You are quick to cage.

You watch, still half asleep,
How dawn mishapes a room;
And all your confidence by the light is drained
And still his face,
His face is still transformed.

JANUARY GLADSONG

Seeing as yet nothing is really well enough arranged,
the dragonfly will not yet sing
nor will the guests ever arrive
quite as naked as the tulips intended.
Still, because once again I am wholly glad of living,
I will make all that is possible step out of time
to a land of giant hurrays! where the happy monsters dance
and stomp darkness down.

Because joy and sorrow must finally unite and the small heart-
beat of sparrow be heard above jet-roar, I will sing
not of tomorrow's impossible paradise
but of what now radiates.
Forever the wind is blowing the white clouds in someone's pure
                                                    direction;
In all our time birdsong has teemed and couples known
that darkness is not forever.
In the glad boat we sail the gentle and invisible ocean
where none have ever really drowned.

ROAD SONG

This evening at least I do not care
where the journey will be ending;
only a landscape softened now
by song and slow rainfall fills me.

The rest of things, her body crushed
against the whitest pillows, regrets
and the more concrete failures
are exiled and done with.

There is nowhere specially to get to.
The towns are identical, each one passed
takes deeper into evening
what sorrows I've brought with me.

In my head some voice is singing
a song that once linked us;
it has ceased to be of importance;
another song might replace it.

Now only my gawky shadow occupies
these roads going nowhere,
that by small towns are linked
and that by the darkness are cancelled.

WHEN INTO SUDDEN BEDS

When through absence into sudden beds
You fall to ward
Off darkness and to share
For habit's sake some human warmth,

If who is now gone in dream returns
To ignite some loss and make
The hand that reaches seem
Blind, ignorant of your suffering,

Then, with a larger sympathy than once you owned,
Must you now turn, elst all dark is yours
And beds, forever blind,
Will make within them wars.

Whatever's touched, shoulder, thigh or breast,
With some uncommon pain will burn
When for love you're asked to pay in kind,
And find you are not large enough to turn.

POEM WRITTEN IN THE STREET
ON A RAINY EVENING

Everything I lost was found again.
I tasted wine in my mouth.
My heart was like a firefly; it moved
Through the darkest objects laughing.

There were enough reasons why this was happening
But I never stopped to think about them.
I could have said it was your face,
Could have said I'd drunk something idiotic,

But no one reason was sufficient,
No one reason was relevant;
My joy was gobbled up by dull surroundings
But there was enough of it.

A feast was spread; a world
Was suddenly made edible.
And there was forever to taste it.

'TONIGHT I WILL NOT BOTHER YOU'

Tonight I will not bother you with telephones
Or voices speaking their cold and regular lines;
I'll write no more notes in crowded living-rooms
Saying what and how much has changed,
But fall instead to silence and things known.

There is no frantic hurry to love
Or press on another one's own dream.
This much I know has changed,
What was once wild is calmed,
And quieter now behind the brain
May throw more light on things;
And what starved for love survives
Whatever breast it hunted down.

When tired of things you scream, throw up
Sorrow that's become a physical pain,
I'll not try and comfort you with words
That add little but darkness to ourselves
But with the body speak, its senses known;
For what faith I have is buried in your breast
Or dreams alone in quiet streets;
It has no rage or philosophy,
No wish to change other than the nearest shapes.

Taking what love comes makes
All that comes much easier;
Something buried deep selects what our shapes need;
The smaller habits it allows to breathe then fade,
Leaving the centre clean.

Tonight I will not bother you with excuses.
If owning separate worlds pain
Comes more easily and hurt
Remains a common part of us,
Then silence is best; it will allow
All doubts to strip themselves.

IT IS TIME TO TIDY UP YOUR LIFE

It is time to tidy up your life!
Into your body has leaked this message.
No conscious actions, no broodings
Have brought the thought upon you.
It is time to take into account
What has gone and what has replaced it.
Living your life according to no plan,
The decisions are numerous and
The ways to go are one.

You stand between trees this evening;
The cigarette in your cupped hand
Glows like a flower.
The drizzle falling seems
To wash away all ambition.
There are scattered through your life
Too many dreams to entirely gather.

Through the soaked leaves, the soaked grasses,
The earth-scents and distant noises
This one thought is re-occurring:
It is time to take into account what has gone,
To cherish and replace it.
You learnt early enough that celebrations
Do not last forever.
So what use now the sorrows that mount up?

You must withdraw your love from that
Which would kill your love.
There is nothing flawless anywhere,
Nothing that has not the power to hurt.
As much as hate, tenderness is the weapon of one
Whose love is neither perfect nor complete.

TRISTAN, WAKING IN HIS WOOD, PANICS

Do not let me win again, not this time,
Not again. I've won too often and know
What winning is about. I do not want to possess;
I do not want to. I will not want you.

Every time a thing is won,
Every time a thing is owned,
Every time a thing is possessed,
It vanishes.

Only the need is perfect, only the wanting.
Tranquillity does not suit me;
I itch for disasters.

I know the seasons; I'm familiar with
Those things that come and go,
Destroy, build up, burn and freeze me.

I'm familiar with opposites
And taste what I can.
But I still stay starving.

It would be easy to blame an age,
Blame fashions that infiltrate and cause
What was thought constant to change.

But what future if I admitted to no dream beyond the one
From which I'm just woken?
Already in the wood the light grass has darkened.

Like a necklace of deaths the flowers hug the ground;
Their scents, once magically known,
Seem now irretrievable.

III
ODD POEMS

INTERRUPTION AT THE OPERA HOUSE

At the very beginning of an important symphony,
while the rich and famous were settling into their quietly
                                        expensive boxes,
a man came crashing through the crowds,
carrying in his hand a cage in which
the rightful owner of the music sat,
yellow and tiny and very poor;
and taking onto the rostrum this rather timid bird
he turned up the microphones, and it sang.

'A very original beginning to the evening,' said the crowds,
quietly glancing at their programmes to find
the significance of the intrusion.

Meanwhile at the box office, the organizers of the evening
were arranging for small and uniformed attendants
to evict, even forcefully, the intruders.
But as the attendants, poor and gathered from the nearby
                                        slums at little expense,
went rushing down the aisles to do their job
they heard, above the coughing and irritable rattling of jewels,
a sound that filled their heads with light,
and from somewhere inside them there bubbled up a stream,
and there came a breeze on which their youth was carried.
How sweetly the bird sang!

And though soon the fur-wrapped crowds
were leaving their boxes and in confusion were winding their
                                        way home
still the attendants sat in the aisles,
and some, so delighted at what they heard, rushed out to call
their families and friends.

And their children came,
sleepy for it was late in the evening,
very late in the evening,
and they hardly knew if they had done with dreaming
or had begun again.
In all the tenement blocks
the lights were clicking on,
and the rightful owner of the music,
tiny and no longer timid, sang
for the rightful owners of the song.

THE LAST RESIDENTS

Mayakovsky, sitting at your window one afternoon,
Half-crazy with sorrow, Your soul finally shipwrecked,
What if you had decided to be foolish,
To be neither cynical nor over-serious,
In fact, not to care?

Would Russia have changed much?
The snows melted in Siberia?
The bright posters propagate a different message?
Would the winter birds, numbed in their trees,
Not have fallen?
Would they have re-raised their heads singing?

These years later I sit at a window in London and see
The same events occurring;
Quieter, more subtly now
Are the prisons fed, the warrants issued.
And the end still seems the same,
The outcome as inevitable.

And no matter how much I care,
Having both love and hatred,
I still see the stars turn negative,
And the last residents of London
Crumble among the plagued allotments
Crying out,
Crying with disbelief and amazement.

She's pulled down the blinds now, she's locking the door,
a unicorn's just stepped down from the wall;
naked as snow on the eiderdown
it's rested its head and its horn.

She's pulled down the blinds now, it's warmer inside,
naked she crosses the room;
the eiderdown's blue and her hair is blonde
and white is the unicorn.

Dreaming, though both far from sleep,
both head and body spin around,
and humming deep into her veins
moves now the unicorn.

Frightened once by normal flesh
her body disallowed
ordinary shapes to entertain her,
even buried deep in dreams —

for touched too soon in hurrying rooms,
the walls, forests they became,
and into myth she faded,
leaf-eyed; birds sang inside her brain.

She's pulled down the blinds now, she's locked the door,
fists bunched tight against a wall;
the eiderdown's blue and her hair is blonde
and red now the unicorn.

ALBATROSS RAMBLE

I woke this morning to find an albatross staring at me.
Funny, it wasn't there last night.
Last night I was alone.

The albatross lay on the bed.
The sheets were soaking.

I live miles from any coast.
I invited no mad sailors home.
I dreamt of no oceans.

The bird is alive, it watches me carefully.
I watch it carefully.
For some particular reason I think
Maybe we deserve one another.

It's sunny outside, spring even.
The sky is bright; it is alive.

I remember I have someone to meet,
Someone clear, someone with whom I'm calm,
Someone who lets things glow.

As I put on my overcoat to go out
I think that maybe after all
I don't deserve this bird.

Albatrosses cause hang-ups.
There's not much I can do with them.
I can't give them in to zoos.
The attendants have enough albatrosses.

Nobody is particularly eager to take it from me.

Maybe, I think, the bird's in the wrong house.
Maybe it meant to go next door.
Maybe some sailor lives next door.
Maybe it belongs to the man upstairs.
Maybe it belongs to the girls in the basement.
It must belong to someone.

I rush into the corridor and shout:
'Does anyone own an albatross? Has anyone lost it?
There's an albatross in my room!'

I'm met by an awkward silence.

I know the man upstairs is not happy.
I know the girls in the basement wander lost among the furniture.
Maybe they're trying to get rid of it
And won't own up.
Maybe they've palmed the albatross off on me.

I don't want an albatross; I don't want this bird;
I've got someone to meet,
Someone patient, someone good and healthy,
Someone whose hands are warm and whose grin
Makes everything babble and say yes.
I'd not like my friend to meet the albatross.

It would eat those smiles;
It would bother that patience;
It would peck at those hands
Till they turned sour and ancient.

Although I have made albatross traps,
Although I have sprayed the thing with glue,
Although I have fed it every poison available,
It still persists in living,
This bird with peculiar shadows
Cast its darkness over everything.

If I go out it would only follow.
It would flop in the seat next to me on the bus,
Scowling at the passengers.
If I took it to the park it would only bother the ducks,
Haunt couples in rowing boats,
Tell the trees it's winter.
It would be patted by policemen as they gently asked:
'Have you an albatross licence?'

Gloom bird, doom bird,
I can do nothing about it.
There are no albatross-exterminators in the directory;
I looked for hours.

Maybe it will stay with me right through summer;
Maybe it has no intentions of leaving.
I'll grow disturbed with this bird never leaving,
This alien bird with me all the time.

And now my friend is knocking on the door,
Less patient, frowning,
A bit sad and angry.

I'll sit behind this door and make noises like an albatross.
A terrible crying.
I'll put my mouth to the keyhole and wail albatross wails.
My friend will know then
I have an albatross in my room.
My friend will sympathize with me,
Go away knowing it's not my fault I can't open the door.

I'll wait here; I might devise some plan:
It's spring and everything is good but for this.
This morning I woke with an albatross in my room.
There's nothing much I can do about it until it goes away.

SPRING SONG

I thought the tree was rather ordinary until yesterday
when seven girls in orange swim-wear climbed into its branches.
Laughing and giggling they unstrapped each other,
letting their breasts fall out,
running fourteen nipples along the branches.
I sat at my window watching.
'Hey,' I said, 'what are yous doing up there?'
'We are coaxing out the small green buds earlier than usual,'
said the first.
Then the second slid down the tree — amazing how brown the
                                                        body was —
and naked she lay on the dead clumpy soil for an hour or more.
On rising there was a brilliant green shape of grass
and the beginning of daisies.

'Are you Spring?' I asked.
'Yes,' she replied. 'And the others also, they are Spring.'
I should have guessed.
What other season permits such nakedness?

The others came in through the window then.
All the dust the room had gathered vanished.
They are the happy gardeners;
their long backs bend to gather cartloads of sadness
and take it elsewhere.

They'll walk among us making our touch perfect.
Their beauty more awkward than even the topmost models,
they'll take our hearts to the laundry
and there'll be but joy in whatever rooms we wake.
We'll love all in that country
where couples glow brilliant
and the craziest amongst them find in their bodies
    promise of laughter.

FULL CIRCLE

It must be upsetting to be a prophet.
It must be embarrassing.
Specially around now, specially now,
It must be unnerving.

What can a prophet say? How can
he not look ridiculous?
It's not a time for prophets, specially now,
specially around now.

Who'd believe him anyway?
Who'd believe if it he said
numerous miracles are about to happen.
We live in a time without miracles.

Maybe that's why it's embarrassing.
In a smug time, in a time without astonishment,
in a time that's done away with wonder.
It must be unnerving.

It must be upsetting also to have
much of passion, to move through a city,
awake, jubilant, to move when
all about disasters are occurring.

What can you do then, what can
you possibly do besides
accept your own freakishness?
And of course you would accept it,

You would accept it wholly
if you knew the outcome,
If you knew somewhere there was
a prophet to forecast the outcome.

SCHOOL NOTE

In the dormitories the well-bred meat
is tucked away.
Safely for the evening
the rich little balls of meat
are tucked away.

Outside in the drive-way
the master's Rolls also sleeps,
a fat beetle among the trees,
shiny and silent it sleeps.

In the dormitories the well-bred meat
moves from the blankets.
Delighted to be left alone,
in hushed voices it chatters,
excited by the darkness.

You can hear the meat rustle out of its nightwear.
Tiptoeing round the beds,
the quiet meat playing.

Some portions, disdainful
of the giggles and the daring,
listen deep into invention.

On itself the meat will practise daring games.
The lanky meat, the coy meat,
the round and innocent meat,
curious to discover
why it is so excitable.

THE LITERARY GATHERING

In those rooms I became more distant than ever.
Where once I went with my head down,
Mumbling answers to obscure questions,
I felt a total stranger.

Poem-freak!
I felt I'd perverted imagination.
I had no real answers.
I'd left my brain at home preserved in lime.

Like a dumb canary let out of its cage
I'd found another cage.
It did not suit me.
In my beak the invitations melted.

Standing there I shook from sleep
What into sleep escaped.
I glanced around the books for friends,
Found only breasts dressed in the latest fashion.

Those for who I sang were not there,
But were instead outside, and laughing drunk
Climbed railings in some public park,
Not caring where it was they went.

Outside again I was alive again.
I begged my soul to be anonymous, to breathe
Free of obscure ambitions and the need
To explain away any song.

THE GIANT SEEN

I stretch beside the body of morning.
A lark's in my fist.
In the clear lake's bottom
My feet are resting.

My hair, blown outwards, is wrapped round clouds.
I do not stalk anything.
Centre-ways between ground and lightning
My stomach rumbles. My sight is not blocked by mountains.
I can gaze into the sun forever.

I bestow everything upon everything : land,
Oceans, air-streams and seasons,
The rest.
I don't know where I get it all from.

There is something in the background whispering
That has never stopped whispering,
Letting me be ;
Under the camouflage of planets
It wags a tongue.

I stretch beside the body of morning,
The pressure that shapes a rose :
Solid, to the senses at least,
Tangible.
The valleys hung upside down
Wait now till I am recognized.

WITHOUT KNOWING MUCH ABOUT IT

One evening when the streams ran loudly
I went into a wood with two friends
Whose differences and arguments were genuine.
I had no idea what it was they were hunting.
One shouted out that the trees were glowing;
The other disagreed, insisted
Nothing had begun yet.

Between their arguments I wandered saying nothing;
In my head some minor pain was growing.
Aware now of the contradictions
Their blood inherits,
Of the forces that through them were moving,
Fifteen and uncertain,
I was smacked awake by loving.

Maybe some parable we'd found
Has set our heads alight.
Adventurous children,
What did we hope to find,
Not long before all directions vanished
And the leaves, glowing with both frost and sunlight,
Fell invisible about us?

THE PESSIMISTIC SONG

It's nearly completed . . .
I walk down the road a little drunk,
not thinking of as much as undressing
the girls going on before me.

It's nearly completed.
I've believed enough in all the webs of beauty,
the soft evenings, the tastes and sweet noises;
I've believed in them.
But what does that alter?

Like the grass that is restless and would go
to where the wind does, I wish to go,
a stream, a river, a continuous dancer knowing nothing,
on no particular stage, without audience.

The dreams, the possessions, the long bodies already surrendered
the longings that build their houses in tomorrow,
they're all in a sack and tied up together.

Fling them away then. . . . They're chains now.
Or bottle up the memories, the bright bubbles;
drink them in the evening when you're restless.
You'll soon be warm and drowsy.

It's nearly completed . . .
The blood brims with oxygens; it reflects
in the flesh that loves have illuminated;
it burns, burns deeply; it's nearly completed.

MEAT

Some pretty little thoughts,
some wise little songs,
some neatly packed observations,
some descriptions of peacocks, of sunsets,
some fat little tears,
something to hold to chubby breasts,
something to put down,
something to sigh about,
I don't want to give you these things.
I want to give you meat,
the splendid meat,
the blemished meat.
Say, here it is,
here is the active ingredient,
the thing that bothers history,
that bothers priest and financier.
Here is the meat.

The sirens wailing on police-cars,
the ambulances alert with pain,
the bricks falling on the young
queens in night-parks
demand meat,
the real thing.

I want to give you something
that bleeds as it leaves my hand
and enters yours,
something that by its rawness,
that by its bleeding
demands to be called real.

In the morning, when you wake,
the sheets are blood-soaked.

For no apparent reason
they're soaked in blood.
Here is the evidence you have been waiting for.
Here is the minor relevation.

A fly made out of meat lands
on a wall made out of meat.
There is meat in the pillows we lie on.
The eiderdowns are full of meat.
I want to give it you
share the headache of the doctor
bending irritated by the beds
as he deals out the hushed truth about the meat,
the meat that can't be saved,
that's got to end,
that's going to be tossed away.

You can strip the meat,
you can sit on it,
you can caress and have sex with it —
the thing that carries its pain around,
that's born in pain,
that lives in pain,
that eats itself to keep itself in pain.

My neighbours driving away in their cars
are moody and quiet and do not talk to me.
I want to fill their cars with meat,
stuff it down their televisions,
leave it in the laundromat
where the shy secretaries gather.

Repetitive among the petals,
among the songs repetitive,
I want the stuff to breathe its name,
the artery to open up and whisper,
I am the meat,
the sole inventor of paradise.

I am the thing denied entrance into heaven,
awkward and perishable,
the most neglected of mammals.
I am the meat that glitters,
that weeps over its temporariness.

I want the furniture to turn into meat,
the door handle as you touch it
to change into meat.

The meat you are shy to take home to mother,
the meat you are,
gone fat and awkward.
Hang it above your bed,
in the morning when you wake drowsy,
find it in the wash-basin.
Nail it to the front door.
In the evening leave it out on the lawns.
The meat that thinks the stars are white flies.
Let the dawn traveller find it among hedgrows,
waiting to offer itself as he passes.
Leave it out among the night-patrols and the lovers.
Leave it between the memorandums of politicians.

Here is the active ingredient;
here is the thing that bothers history,
that bothers priest and financier.
Pimply and blunt and white,
it comes towards you with its hands outstretched.
How you love the meat.